THANK YOU FOR BEING HERE.

The purpose of this magazine is multifaceted. We identify and address the specific needs and barriers faced by returning citizens during the reintegration process. Through comprehensive articles, features, and expert insights, we aim to shed light on the challenges and opportunities that lie ahead, providing guidance and support along the way.

1 TAPPED-IN Magazine will serve as a comprehensive resource hub, reporting on the joint events, workshops, and training sessions organized by the RCA. We will share information on these valuable opportunities for personal development and empowerment, ensuring that returning citizens are equipped with the knowledge and skills necessary to thrive in society.

2 The proceeds from subscriptions will assist the RCA in developing and delivering educational programs that cater to the unique needs of returning citizens. By highlighting educational initiatives, success stories, and providing access to scholarships and resources, we aim to foster a pathway towards academic achievement and long-term success.

3 The readers will have access to personal stories, interviews, and documentaries that not only highlight successful reintegration but also provide positive role models for returning citizens. By featuring individuals who have overcome challenges and achieved personal growth, we seek to inspire and motivate others to strive for greatness in their own lives.

4 The RCA will develop and implement programs that address the specific needs of returning citizens, including housing, employment, healthcare, education, and social support. By sharing resources, expertise, and best practices in the field of reintegration and support services, we aim to create a network of support and collaboration that uplifts and empowers returning citizens across the nation.

TAPPED-IN Magazine is more than just a publication. It is a beacon of hope, a source of knowledge, and a catalyst for change. We invite you to join us on this transformative journey as we tap into the untapped potential of returning citizens and contribute to a more inclusive and compassionate society.

RETURNING CITIZENS ASSOCIATION

Richard Gaines

Executive Director

Andrea Gaines

Treasurer

Nina Clark

Secretary/Community Liaison

Marcus Sanders

Project Director

Denise Coleman

Project Director

Jesse Pitts

Project Director

Dear Readers,

It is with great excitement and gratitude that I welcome you to the second edition of Tapped-In Magazine! This publication is more than just a magazine—it's a platform for transformation, a celebration of resilience, and a testament to the strength of system-impacted individuals and communities.

Resilience is about navigating challenges, overcoming barriers, and emerging stronger, with a deeper understanding of our purpose. Since the release of our first edition, we have been inspired by the stories of courage, creativity, and empowerment from our contributors and readers. In this edition, you'll find powerful testimonials, stunning visual art, and captivating storytelling that embody the theme of education.

This past year has been a transformative one for RCA. We've expanded our programs, strengthened our partnerships, and deepened our commitment to providing holistic support for returning citizens. Our weekly non-clinical mental health support groups, mentorship programs, and resilience-building initiatives have reached new heights, thanks to your unwavering support. Your continued engagement and support remind us that our mission matters. Together, we can build a future where every returning citizen has the opportunity to thrive.

Thank you for being part of this journey. I hope this edition inspires, challenges, and uplifts you.

In solidarity,

Richard Gaines
Executive Director
Returning Citizens Association

CONTENTS

The Power of Education:
Unlocking Potential

Spotlight on Richard Gaines, Founder and Executive Director of RCA

Education is one of the most transformative forces in the world—a tool that can break barriers, reshape futures, and unlock the hidden potential within individuals who society may have counted out. For system-impacted individuals, education offers more than knowledge; it provides hope, resilience, and a path to personal empowerment. Few embody this truth more powerfully than Richard Gaines, Founder and Executive Director of the Returning Citizens Association (RCA).

Having spent 24 years incarcerated, Richard's journey from confinement to leadership is a testament to the transformative power of education and perseverance. His unwavering commitment to personal growth and helping others has shaped RCA into a beacon of support for system-impacted individuals.

Education Behind Bars: Transforming Adversity into Opportunity

While serving a 29-year-to-life sentence, Richard found education to be a lifeline. Determined to transform his life, he earned an Associate of Arts degree from Patten University between 2006 and 2010. Education, for Richard, wasn't just about acquiring knowledge—it was a way to reclaim his identity and begin envisioning a future beyond prison walls. "Education gave me the tools to redefine who I was," Richard reflects. "It became the foundation for everything I've done since, both personally and professionally."

Richard didn't stop at his own education. He began sharing his knowledge with others, mentoring fellow incarcerated individuals and facilitating workshops on resilience and personal growth. These early experiences planted the seeds for what would later become RCA, an organization devoted to uplifting others through education, mentorship, and advocacy.

The Birth of the Returning Citizens Association

In 2022, Richard founded the Returning Citizens Association (RCA) in Oakland, California, with the vision of supporting system-impacted individuals and their families. RCA was built on a simple but powerful philosophy: "Nothing About Us Without Us." The organization's programs are shaped by the lived experiences of those who understand the challenges of reentry firsthand.

Richard's leadership and RCA's innovative approach quickly gained traction, and in 2024, RCA achieved federal tax-exempt 501(c)(3) status, solidifying its role as a vital resource for system-impacted individuals nationwide.

Education in Action:
Empowering Others to Succeed

After his release in 2019, Richard continued to build on the foundation he had created while incarcerated. He furthered his education at Laney College and applied his skills in social services, eventually serving as a case manager at the Felton Institute in San Francisco. These experiences prepared him to lead RCA, where his focus remains on empowering others to reclaim their stories and rebuild their lives. Under Richard's leadership, RCA offers programs that include:

• The Reentry Mentorship Program, providing one-on-one support for individuals navigating reentry.
• The Youth Resilience Mentorship Program, designed to inspire and empower the next generation.
• Tapped-In Magazine, a groundbreaking publication amplifying the voices of system-impacted individuals.

The Ripple Effect of Education

Richard's story is a powerful reminder of the ripple effect that education can create. His personal transformation has inspired countless others to pursue their own paths of growth and empowerment. RCA's impact extends beyond individuals, strengthening families and communities by offering the tools and support needed for lasting success.

"Education doesn't just change one life; it creates opportunities for generations. It's a way to rewrite the narrative for families, communities, and society as a whole."

Looking Ahead: A Vision for Growth

As RCA continues to expand its reach, Richard remains focused on creating programs that address the unique challenges faced by system-impacted individuals. With federal 501(c)(3) status in place, RCA is poised to secure additional funding, form new partnerships, and deepen its impact across the country.

Education is more than a pathway to success—it's a catalyst for transformation. Richard Gaines's journey from incarceration to leadership is proof that with determination and access to resources, anyone can unlock their potential and build a brighter future. Through RCA, Richard is not only reclaiming his own story but helping thousands of others do the same. His legacy demonstrates the profound power of education to change lives, challenge stigmas, and create a more equitable society. "Reclaiming Our Lives, Reclaiming Our Stories" isn't just RCA's slogan—it's the mission that drives Richard Gaines and the organization he founded to empower system-impacted individuals to unlock their true potential.

Breaking Barriers in Employment

BUILDING BRIDGES TO SUCCESS

Willie Moffett Jr.'s Vision for Reentry and Community Empowerment

For over 25 years, Willie Moffett Jr. has been a transformative figure in Pittsburg, California, breaking barriers and paving the way for system-impacted individuals to reclaim their lives. As the CEO of the Pittsburg Youth Development Center, Inc., and the orchestrator of the Village Collaborative, Willie has dedicated his life to empowering those who have faced the challenges of life after incarceration. His most recent endeavor, the creation of California Support Services (CSS), co-founded with his son, Willie Moffett III, builds on his life experiences and seeks to redefine second chances. This groundbreaking initiative offers meaningful employment, mentorship, and holistic support to justice-impacted individuals, providing a model for reentry programs nationwide.

The Journey from Incarceration to Leadership

Willie's journey began with a 10-year prison sentence, which transformed his outlook on life. Upon his release in 1999, however, he faced immediate barriers. His parole plans were denied, forcing him to return to the very environment that contributed to his initial incarceration. Parole at the time was not designed to foster reintegration; rather, it perpetuated the cycle of recidivism for many justice-impacted individuals.

CONGRESSMAN GEORGE MILLER VISITING THE PAROLE PROGRAM CREATED BY WILLIE MOFFETT JR.

Willie's determination to break free from this cycle was unwavering. Within three weeks of his release, he began working for a nonprofit organization. Despite the nonprofit facing financial difficulties in 2000—causing 90% of employees to leave—Willie remained. Recognizing an opportunity to build something meaningful, he stayed on, taking on challenges that would eventually lead to his appointment as Operations Manager in 2003.

In this role, Willie began reimagining hiring processes, focusing on providing opportunities for individuals impacted by state, federal, and county prison systems, as well as young adults at risk of incarceration. This vision evolved into The Parolee Program, a model recognized throughout the Bay Area and even by Congressman George Miller, who visited to observe the program firsthand. Willie's guiding principles were clear: "It's not where you're from, it's how you come."

This initiative went beyond employment. Willie provided participants with clothing, housing, and transportation, instilling in them the values of self-respect, a hunger for success, and a commitment to personal growth. His innovative approach transformed lives and laid the foundation for what would eventually become California Support Services.

The Birth of California Support Services

In 2025, Willie Moffett Jr. and his son, Willie Moffett III, launched California Support Services (CSS), a second-chance employment enterprise rooted in Willie's lived experiences and commitment to empowering others. This father-son partnership leveraged years of lessons learned to create a sustainable model that bridges the gap between reentry and long-term success.

CSS provides justice-impacted individuals with meaningful employment opportunities and holistic support systems, ensuring their successful reintegration into society. The initiative also features a key partnership with the Returning Citizens Association (RCA), an organization recognized for its professionalism and ability to mentor and navigate impacted individuals through life's challenges. CSS has contracted RCA members to lead its Mentorship and Navigation Department, ensuring high-quality guidance and support for participants.

Breaking Barriers: Key Elements of CSS

- **Employment Opportunities:** Jobs tailored to participants' skills and needs, offering financial stability and independence.
- **Mentorship:** RCA mentors and reentry specialists provide personalized guidance, resilience training, and professional development.
- **Holistic Support Services:** Participants gain access to housing resources, financial literacy training, and mental health support, addressing the multifaceted challenges of reentry.

Willie emphasizes the significance of these efforts: "This initiative is about more than just jobs. It's about creating pathways to success and showing people that they are capable of achieving their dreams, no matter their past."

The Vision Behind the Village Collaborative

A cornerstone of Willie's leadership is the Village Collaborative, a network of organizations that work together to address the needs of returning citizens, at-risk youth, and families in Pittsburg, California. By pooling resources and expertise, the collaborative has created a powerful support system for those navigating reentry and reintegration.

"When organizations come together with a shared purpose, we can create real, lasting change. The Village Collaborative is proof that we're *stronger together*."

A Legacy of Hope and Empowerment

Looking ahead, Willie remains steadfast in his vision to expand programs like CSS and the Village Collaborative. His dream is to see reentry initiatives in every community, offering justice-impacted individuals the tools and opportunities they need to succeed.

Willie's message to those impacted by the justice system is clear: "Your past does not define your future. Believe in yourself, surround yourself with people who support you, and take every step forward with purpose. Change is possible, and it begins with you."

Through innovative programs, strategic partnerships, and a deep commitment to second chances, Willie Moffett Jr. is transforming lives and communities. His work serves as a testament to the power of resilience, the importance of collaboration, and the enduring impact of creating pathways to success for justice-impacted individuals.

Willie Moffett Jr.'s journey from incarceration to community leader exemplifies the transformative power of vision, perseverance, and service. His work with California Support Services, provides a blueprint for reentry programs that address employment, mentorship, and holistic support. As CSS and its initiatives unfold in 2025, they promise to leave a lasting legacy of empowerment, hope, and resilience for justice-impacted individuals and their families.

Empowering
the Next Generation

RCA's Pilot Youth Mentorship Program in Chico, California

In Chico, California, the Returning Citizens Association (RCA) recently launched an innovative pilot program to engage and support high school students through mentorship and proactive community-building efforts. Recognizing the unique challenges faced by today's youth, RCA designed the Youth Mentorship Program to help students navigate life's obstacles, avoid the pitfalls of systemic challenges, and build a foundation for brighter futures. Overseen by RCA Executive Director Richard Gaines and spearheaded by Marcus Sanders, Project Director and Youth Coordinator, this pilot program represents RCA's first step in establishing a long-term youth-focused initiative in Chico.

The Vision: Building Resilience and Fostering Connection

The goal of the pilot program was twofold:

1. To understand the specific challenges faced by high school students in Chico, particularly those that echo the struggles experienced by justice-impacted individuals.
2. To build trust and relationships with the school and the community, creating a foundation for a comprehensive program in the upcoming semester.

"We wanted to be proactive about addressing the challenges young people face before they escalate into life-altering issues," says Marcus Sanders. "We've been through the system, and our hope is to steer these students away from the mistakes we made and give them the tools they need to succeed."

The Pilot Program in Action

The pilot program ran for several weeks, during which RCA facilitators provided presentations and hosted discussions with high school students. Key focus areas included:

- Values and Decision-Making: Helping students align their values with their actions to make better life choices.
- Resilience Building: Teaching coping strategies and emotional tools to overcome adversity.
- Community and Identity: Encouraging students to reflect on their role in their community and the impact of their choices.

The sessions were interactive and tailored to the needs of the students, with RCA mentors drawing on their own lived experiences to inspire and connect. "It's about more than teaching," says Richard Gaines. "It's about being real with them—showing them that we've been where they are, and there's a better path forward."

Feedback and Impact

The pilot program received overwhelmingly positive feedback from students, educators, and the community. Many students expressed gratitude for the mentors' honesty and authenticity, noting that it was the first time they had engaged in such open and relatable conversations about life's challenges. One student shared, "Hearing their stories made me realize I don't have to follow the same path. I can make better choices now before it's too late."

Teachers and school administrators praised the program for its ability to engage students in meaningful discussions about their futures, and many expressed interest in working with RCA to implement a full-scale program.

Next Steps: Expanding the Vision

Building on the success of the pilot program, RCA plans to launch a semester-long initiative at the high school in Chico. This expanded program will include mentorship sessions, presentations/work-shops on personal development, and community service projects to help students build a sense of purpose and responsibility. "We're committed to making a lasting impact," says Marcus Sanders. "This is just the beginning of a partnership that will empower students to take control of their futures." As RCA continues to grow its Youth Mentorship Program, Chico is poised to become a model for how communities can come together to support their most vulnerable populations—before challenges become crises.

The success of the Chico pilot program demonstrates the importance of early intervention, authentic mentorship, and a commitment to the next generation. RCA looks forward to expanding this initiative, reaching more students, and continuing to build resilient communities across the country.

"It's not just about guiding them away from our mistakes—it's about showing them what's possible when they take charge of their lives and make positive choices."
— Marcus Sanders

ADVOCATES OF GROWTH

Across the country, individuals and organizations are stepping up to challenge the flaws in the criminal justice system and advocate for meaningful change. These advocates bring passion, experience, and resilience to the fight for justice, focusing on policies and programs that create real change for system-impacted individuals and their communities. In this edition of Tapped-In Magazine, we're proud to highlight three advocates whose work is transforming lives and pushing for a more equitable system.

The Power of Advocacy

These advocates are just a few examples of the many individuals working tirelessly to transform the criminal justice system. Their efforts remind us that change begins with action—whether it's mentoring youth, expanding access to resources, or creating opportunities for second chances. Their voices are powerful, their work is inspiring, and their impact is undeniable. Together, they're proving that advocacy isn't just about fighting for change—it's about building a more just and compassionate society.

"Advocacy means taking action. It's about standing up for what's right and creating opportunities for others to thrive." – Richard Gaines, Executive Director, RCA

1. Marcus Sanders: Mentoring the Next Generation

As Project Director and Youth Coordinator for the Returning Citizens Association (RCA), Marcus Sanders has made it his mission to prevent youth from making the same mistakes he did. With lived experience as a system-impacted individual, Marcus uses his story to inspire others and create programs that steer young people toward brighter futures. Recently, Marcus spearheaded RCA's pilot Youth Mentorship Program in Chico, California. By working directly with high school students, he focuses on building resilience, teaching life skills, and encouraging them to make positive choices.

"We can't just talk about change—we have to show up and create it," says Marcus. *"Our youth need guidance, and I'm here to provide it."*

2. Rachel Kinnon: Expanding Access to Information

As the Jail and Reentry Services Manager at the San Francisco Public Library, Rachel Kinnon is breaking down barriers for system-impacted individuals through the power of information. Rachel's work ensures that incarcerated and formerly incarcerated individuals have access to books, resources, and educational materials that can support their reentry and personal growth. Through partnerships with organizations like RCA, Rachel has helped bring initiatives like Tapped-In Magazine into libraries and correctional facilities, amplifying voices that often go unheard.

"The library is for everyone," Rachel emphasizes. *"By sharing stories, art, and information, we're empowering people to rewrite their narratives and build a better future."*

3. Willie Moffett Jr.: Creating Second Chances

Willie Moffett Jr., CEO of California Support Services, is redefining reentry through employment opportunities and mentorship. With over 25 years of experience as a community leader, Willie's work focuses on breaking barriers for returning citizens by providing stable jobs, support networks, and guidance. His newest initiative aims to create second-chance jobs for justice-impacted individuals while offering mentorship and life skills training.

"Employment is more than a paycheck—it's a path to dignity and self-worth," says Willie. *"My goal is to help people rebuild their lives and contribute to their communities."*

Expanding Information Access

How Libraries Empower Growth Through Education

In a world where opportunity isn't always evenly distributed, libraries stand as one of the few places where everyone is welcome. They are more than just buildings filled with books—they are centers of knowledge, empowerment, and connection.

For many people, libraries provide access to resources they might not have at home. Free books open doors to education, self-improvement, and creativity. Public computers help bridge the digital divide, allowing people to apply for jobs, take online courses, and stay informed. Community programs support lifelong learning, from children's storytime sessions to career workshops and financial literacy classes.

But beyond practical resources, libraries offer something deeper—a sense of belonging. They are one of the few places where no one is asking for money, where people of all backgrounds can come together to learn, grow, and dream. *They create a space where knowledge isn't a privilege but a right.*

In an era where technology dominates, libraries remain a sanctuary for reflection and discovery. They remind us that books still hold power, that education is still the great equalizer, and that no matter where you come from, the ability to learn can change your life.

A Path to Freedom Within

To those who find themselves behind bars, a library can be more than just a room full of books—it can be a lifeline. It can be a classroom, a courtroom, and an escape all in one. The world may have locked you away, but your mind remains free, and the key to keeping it that way is knowledge.

Education is one of the most powerful tools for changing your future. Studies show that people who continue learning while incarcerated are far less likely to return to prison after release. Whether it's earning a GED, learning a new trade, learning drawing techniques, or diving into history, prison libraries offer the chance to grow beyond your past and prepare for a better future.

Beyond education, books offer something just as valuable—mental freedom. Through reading, you can escape the four walls around you, exploring new worlds, perspectives, and possibilities. Whether it's a novel that transports you to another life, a self-help book that strengthens your mind, or poetry that reminds you of your humanity, every page is an opportunity to stay connected to yourself and your dreams.

But perhaps one of the most important resources in a prison library is legal knowledge. Many people in the system don't have access to proper legal representation, but books on law and self-advocacy can help you understand your rights, navigate appeals, and fight for yourself. When you know the law, you take back power that others might want to keep from you.

You may not have control over your surroundings right now, but you do have control over what you put into your mind. The library is a door—one that leads to knowledge, freedom, and a future beyond these walls. The only question is: *Will you step through it?*

Scan the QR code to find your local library! To get a library card, be sure to bring a valid form of photo ID.

Financial Literacy 101

Mastering Your Money for a Brighter Future

Financial literacy is a cornerstone of personal and professional success, yet it's a skill many of us weren't taught in school. For system-impacted individuals and those navigating reentry, understanding money management can mean the difference between thriving and struggling. A strong grasp of budgeting, credit management, and long-term planning can provide a foundation for a stable and independent future. Let's dive deeper into these critical financial principles and explore practical strategies for success.

1. The Basics of Budgeting

A budget is your financial blueprint—it shows where your money comes from and where it goes. With a well-constructed budget, you can cover essentials, pay off debt, and even set money aside for future goals. Here's how to get started:

Track Your Income and Expenses
- **List All Income Sources:** Include wages, gig work, public assistance, or any other income. Be sure to calculate your net income (after taxes).
- **Categorize Expenses:** Break down your spending into categories such as rent, utilities, food, transportation, debt payments, and savings. Don't forget smaller, variable expenses like entertainment or coffee.
- **Use a Notebook or App:** Whether you prefer pen and paper or technology, tracking expenses is key.

Set Spending Limits
The 50/30/20 rule is a helpful guide:
- **50% for Needs:** Cover essentials like rent, utilities, groceries, and transportation.
- **30% for Wants:** Enjoy non-essentials like dining out or entertainment, but keep this in check.
- **20% for Savings and Debt Repayment:** Pay off high-interest debt first, and start building an emergency fund.

Be Realistic and Flexible
Life is unpredictable. Regularly review your budget and adjust it to accommodate unexpected expenses or changes in income. Celebrate small victories, like saving $10 extra one month or sticking to your meal-prep plan for a week.

2. Building and Repairing Credit

Good credit is a gateway to opportunities, from better housing and car loans to lower interest rates. For those reentering society or rebuilding finances, these steps can pave the way toward better credit:

Start Small and Build Trust
- **Secured Credit Cards:** These cards require a deposit upfront, which acts as your credit limit. Use them for small, regular purchases and pay off the balance in full every month.
- **Credit Builder Loans:** Offered by some credit unions and online lenders, these loans are designed to establish or repair credit by allowing you to "borrow" money that's kept in a savings account until the loan is repaid.

Pay on Time
- **Set Reminders or Automate Payments:** Missing a payment can stay on your credit report for seven years, so avoid late payments at all costs.
- **Communicate with Lenders:** If you're struggling to make payments, contact your lender to discuss options like deferment or a payment plan.

Manage Credit Utilization
- **Stay Below 30% Utilization:** If your credit limit is $1,000, aim to use no more than $300. Lower utilization rates can boost your credit score.
- **Pay Down Balances:** Even paying an extra $20 a month toward your balance can make a big difference over time.

Monitor Your Credit Report
- **Request Free Reports:** Visit AnnualCreditReport.com to review your credit report for errors or fraudulent activity.
- **Dispute Errors Promptly:** Contact the credit bureaus if you spot inaccuracies. Fixing errors can significantly improve your score.

3. Planning for the Long Term

Financial stability isn't just about today—it's about building a secure future. Even small, consistent efforts can lead to big changes over time.

Create an Emergency Fund
An emergency fund is your financial safety net.
- **Start Small:** Save $5 to $10 weekly, even if your income is limited.
- **Aim Big:** Work toward saving three to six months' worth of living expenses to handle emergencies like car repairs or medical bills.
- **Keep It Accessible:** Use a separate savings account that's easy to access in case of an emergency but separate from your everyday spending account.

Invest Wisely

Investing might seem intimidating, but it's one of the best ways to grow your wealth over time.

- **Employer-Sponsored Retirement Plans:** If your employer offers a 401(k), take advantage of it —especially if they match contributions.
- **Start Small with Index Funds:** These low-cost investments track the overall market and are ideal for beginners.
- **Roth IRAs:** Consider a Roth IRA for tax-free growth and withdrawals during retirement.

Seek Professional Advice

Many nonprofits and community organizations offer free or low-cost financial counseling. A financial advisor can also help you create a customized plan for your goals.

4. Practical Money Management Tips for Everyday Life

Avoid Predatory Practices

- **Watch Out for Payday Loans:** These loans often come with exorbitant interest rates. Explore alternatives like small-dollar loans from credit unions or local assistance programs.
- **Beware of Scams:** Be cautious when sharing financial information, especially online. Trust reputable institutions and verify any requests for money.

Reduce Unnecessary Spending

- **Meal Prep:** Cooking at home is often cheaper and healthier than dining out.
- **Cancel Unused Subscriptions:** Review recurring expenses and eliminate services you don't use.
- **Shop Smart:** Look for sales, use coupons, and consider secondhand items.

Celebrate Milestones

Every step toward financial stability is worth celebrating. Paid off a credit card? Saved $100? Take a moment to recognize your achievement.

Building Confidence Through Financial Knowledge

Mastering financial literacy is a journey, not a destination. Start where you are, take one step at a time, and don't be afraid to ask for help when you need it. The skills and habits you develop today will create a brighter, more secure tomorrow.

Remember:

It's never too late to build a solid financial foundation. By taking control of your money, you're investing in yourself—and that's a decision that always pays off.

By Anthony Partee, RCA Project Director and President of Barca-EL Inc.

THE IMPORTANCE OF CRYPTOCURRENCY

For Returning Citizens

In any society driven by commerce, money serves as the lifeblood. Without it, survival becomes an uphill battle. This reality is starkly evident to those who have risked everything, often finding themselves entangled in the justice system due to economic crimes. For these individuals, adapting to the ever-evolving financial landscape is not just important—it's essential.

The world of finance is in constant flux, with outdated systems giving way to advanced technologies. Money, a cornerstone of human progress, has transformed from seashells and stones to precious metals, paper currency, and now digital assets. As the global economy shifts toward digital currencies like Bitcoin, returning citizens must align themselves with this change to avoid being left behind.

The Evolution of Money
For centuries, humans have used various forms of currency to facilitate trade—seashells, stones, copper, gold, and diamonds. The 13th-century Chinese introduction of fiat paper money marked a monumental shift, later adopted by nations like the United States. However, fiat money, created with minimal effort, often leads to economic instability.

Enter Bitcoin, a revolutionary form of currency regarded as the greatest financial innovation of our time. Unlike traditional money, Bitcoin is:
Portable: Send it anywhere globally within minutes.
Borderless: No government can block transactions.
Permissionless: No bank account or approval is required to participate.
Decentralized: It operates independently of central authorities, making it immune to shutdowns.
Divisible and Scarce: With a cap of 21 million bitcoins, its scarcity ensures increased value over time.

Why Bitcoin Matters
For years, influential figures dismissed Bitcoin as a scam. Take Jamie Dimon, CEO of JPMorgan Chase, who once stated anyone buying Bitcoin within his company would be fired. Today, JPMorgan supports Bitcoin-based financial products. Similarly, Larry Fink, CEO of Black-Rock—the world's largest asset manager—called Bitcoin an "index of money laundering" in 2017. Now, Fink actively promotes Bitcoin ETFs.

These leaders amassed Bitcoin while dissuading others, only to later profit from selling it through financial products. The issue? Buying Bitcoin through ETFs gives you fiat currency, while entities like BlackRock keep the actual Bitcoin, leaving retail investors holding paper claims instead of the real asset.

The Opportunity for Returning Citizens
Bitcoin's potential for wealth creation is unprecedented. Imagine an asset priced at $100,000 today that could rise to $1 million in five years—a 10x return. Twenty or thirty years down the line, the same asset could be worth $10–$20 million. This is not hype but a reflection of Bitcoin's scarcity and increasing demand.

For returning citizens, Bitcoin represents a chance to participate in the greatest wealth transfer in history. The barriers to entry are minimal, and the opportunities are vast, but awareness and education are key. Fear of the unknown often holds us back, but in this case, the greater risk lies in not participating.

Bitcoin as a Path to Financial Empowerment
The opportunity to redefine your financial future is here. Bitcoin offers system-impacted individuals a pathway to economic independence, free from the constraints of traditional systems. However, understanding and navigating this space requires education, awareness, and a willingness to embrace change.

The financial world is evolving, and Bitcoin is at the forefront of this revolution. It's not just a currency; it's a tool for empowerment. For returning citizens, this could be a stepping stone toward rebuilding their lives and securing their futures.

This is not financial advice but is provided for educational purposes only. Contact me for more info:

Anthony Partee
www.barca-elinc.in
anthonypartee@barca-elinc.in

BREAKING THE STIGMA

Supporting Returning Citizens and Fostering Understanding

When a loved one reenters society after incarceration, the journey is often challenging—not just for them, but for their families and communities as well. Breaking the stigma surrounding system-impacted individuals is essential to creating a supportive environment that fosters growth, dignity, and second chances. Andrea Gaines, a family member of a system-impacted individual, Ricky Gaines, and an advocate for reentry reform, shares her lived experience and practical tips for wives, families and communities looking to support returning citizens.

Understanding the Stigma

"Stigma is one of the biggest barriers to reentry," Andrea explains. "It affects how people see themselves and how they're treated by society." Returning citizens often face judgment, limited opportunities, and exclusion, making it harder to rebuild their lives. For families and communities, addressing this stigma starts with understanding its roots:

Fear of the Unknown: Misconceptions about those who've been incarcerated often lead to fear/mistrust.

Stereotypes: Media and societal narratives often paint returning citizens in a negative light, reinforcing harmful biases.

Lack of Awareness: Many people don't understand the systemic challenges that returning citizens face, from employment discrimination to limited access to housing and education.

Tips for Families: Building Bridges of Support

For Andrea, supporting her loved one during reentry was a journey of patience, education, and empathy. Here are her tips for families navigating this process:

1. Start with Compassion

"It's important to see your loved one as a human being. Someone who has emotions desires and their own experiences. Emotional support during this time can make the difference, helping them feel secure and motivated to continue their journey of growth. It's OK to not be OK. Create a safe space for them to express themselves and reassure them that they are not alone." Andrea shares.

Compassion means recognizing that the reentry journey will have its ups and downs. There may be moments of frustration or setbacks, but it's important to focus on progress rather than perfection. putting yourself in their shoes and acknowledging the courage it takes to rebuild a life after incarceration.

2. Be Patient with the Process

Reentry is not a straightforward journey—it's a process filled with progress, setbacks, and learning curves. Patience is essential, both for your loved one and for yourself. Understand that adjusting to life after incarceration takes time, as they navigate new routines, responsibilities, and challenges. It's important to manage your expectations and recognize that change doesn't happen overnight.

Andrea emphasizes the importance of patience. "Understanding that everything will not happen all at once. Its ok to put one foot in front of the other and take your time as this is a journey not a destination. Celebrate and bask in the fact that your loved one is no longer in prison." she shares. By being patient, you allow your loved one the space to grow at their own pace, free from the pressure of unrealistic expectations.

Equally important is practicing patience with yourself. Supporting someone through reentry can be emotionally taxing, and there will be moments of frustration or uncertainty. Give yourself grace and remember that your love, understanding, and steady presence can be a powerful source of strength for both you and your loved one.

3. Practice Gratitude and Thankfulness

Amid the challenges of reentry, it's important to focus on the positives and express gratitude for the progress being made. Take time to acknowledge the small wins and the efforts your loved one is putting into rebuilding their life. Gratitude not only fosters a positive atmosphere but also reminds both you and your loved one of the strength and resilience that exists within your relationship.

Andrea highlights how being thankful can shift perspectives during difficult times. "I maintained a grateful and thankful attitude which has helped me shift my perspective and mood no matter what the situation or circumstances I was experiencing. Honoring God and this second chance/opportunity to rebuild and to connection was at the center," she shares. Recognizing the growth in your loved one and the steps forward, no matter how small, helps reinforce their sense of worth and keeps the focus on hope and possibility. This gratitude can also extend to the resources, programs, or individuals who support you and your loved one during this process. Whether it's a counselor, a support group, or a friend offering encouragement, acknowledging these contributions strengthens your support network and reminds you that you're not navigating this journey alone.

"Support starts with empathy and grows with action. Together, we can create a world where second chances aren't just a possibility— they're a reality."

4. Educate Yourself & Seek Community

Learn about the challenges returning citizens face, from systemic barriers to emotional struggles. This knowledge can help you offer better support and advocate for their needs. Look for local organizations, like the Returning Citizens Association (RCA), that offer mentorship, job training, and mental health support. Connecting your loved one with these resources can ease their transition.

5. Communicate Openly & Encourage Growth

Create a safe space for honest conversations. "Ask how you can support them, and be willing to listen without judgment," Andrea advises. Support their goals, whether it's pursuing education, finding employment, or reconnecting with the community. Celebrate their successes, no matter how small.

Tips for Communities: Fostering Understanding and Inclusion

Communities play a vital role in breaking the stigma and creating opportunities for returning citizens to thrive. Andrea emphasizes the importance of collective action:

1. Challenge Stereotypes & Advocate for Change

Speak out against negative narratives about system-impacted individuals. "Language matters," Andrea says. "Using terms like 'returning citizen' instead of 'ex-convict' can shift perceptions and promote dignity and remind others that returning citizens are people."

2. Create Opportunities & Foster Inclusion

Host community events or workshops to raise awareness about reentry challenges and how the community can help.

3. Create Welcoming Spaces

Help eturning citizens feel valued and connected. "A sense of belonging can make all the difference," Andrea says.

Breaking the Cycle Through Understanding

Andrea's journey as a family member of a system-impacted individual taught her the importance of breaking down barriers and building bridges. "Reentry is a family and community effort," she explains. "When we work together to create understanding and opportunity, we give people the tools they need to succeed—and that benefits all of us."

A Call to Action

As families and communities, we have the power to transform the reentry experience from one of judgment to one of possibility. By breaking the stigma and fostering understanding, we can empower returning citizens to reclaim their lives and build a brighter future.

12/14/24 Building Resilience Act 13
San Francisco Public Library

Nina Clark – A Voice of Resilience

Nina Clark's journey is one of transformation, courage, and advocacy. As the Community Liaison and Secretary for the Returning Citizens Association (RCA), Nina uses her voice and lived experiences to inspire and empower others. Her story, shaped by challenges and triumphs, is a testament to the strength of resilience and the power of healing through advocacy and community.

Early Life and the Path to Advocacy

Born and raised in Oakland, Nina's childhood was filled with joy and diversity, growing up in a close-knit community she fondly remembers as a "colorblind" neighborhood. However, her teenage years marked the beginning of her battle with domestic violence. A series of abusive relationships, starting at just 14, deeply impacted her sense of self-worth and safety. Despite these hardships, Nina's inner strength and determination to reclaim her life led her to break the cycle of violence.

"Domestic violence is traumatizing, but it gave me the courage to speak up for myself and others. I refused to let it define my future."

Finding Her Voice and Helping Others

Nina's experiences ignited a passion for advocacy. She began sharing her story through public speaking, partnering with organizations like the San Francisco Police Department to raise awareness about domestic violence. "I started telling people my story, writing about it, and even performing spoken word poetry," Nina explains. "It gave me strength and helped other women find their own courage."

Her powerful poem, simply titled *Domestic Violence,* has moved countless women to tears and inspired them to seek help. Nina's ability to connect with others on such a raw and emotional level is one of her greatest strengths.

Joining RCA and Expanding Her Impact

In 2019, Nina met Ricky Gaines, RCA's Executive Director, through her work in mental health services. Recognizing her passion for helping others, Ricky invited Nina to join RCA. What began as a discussion about the groundbreaking Tapped-In Magazine quickly grew into a larger role as Nina became a key member of RCA's leadership team.

"RCA has given me so much motivation," Nina says. "It started with the magazine, but now we're building programs, supporting communities, and changing lives. Seeing this vision come to life in real time is the most rewarding experience."

Nina has played an integral role in RCA's growth, from organizing mentorship programs to fostering connections with system-impacted individuals and their families. Her commitment to building resilience within the community is unwavering.

A Champion for Survivors and Advocates

Nina's work at RCA is deeply informed by her own journey. She advocates for early intervention and education to prevent domestic violence and helps survivors find their voice and heal. "Healing begins when you speak out and connect with others who understand," she says.

Nina envisions RCA expanding its reach by creating a domestic violence support group specifically for system-impacted women. "Even if it helps just one person, it's worth it," she says. "Women need to know they're not alone and that they have the strength to overcome."

Looking Ahead

In 2025, Nina is focused on developing resources for RCA's programs and empowering others through story-telling and public speaking. She is also excited about the upcoming expansion of Tapped-In Magazine, which she believes will continue to inspire and uplift incarcerated individuals across the country.

When asked about her message to readers, Nina says, "Resilience is about never giving up. You'll face storms, but the light is at the end of the tunnel. Keep going, keep fighting, and know you're not alone."

A Legacy of Hope and Empowerment

Nina Clark's journey from survivor to advocate exemplifies the mission of RCA: reclaiming lives and rewriting narratives. Her story continues to inspire countless individuals to find their voice, seek help, and build a brighter future.

Nina's unwavering commitment to helping others reminds us all of the ripple effect of resilience—when one person heals, entire families and communities benefit. In her own words, "We've been through so much, but we're still here. That's what resilience is all about."

"Believe in yourself and never stop pushing forward. Surround yourself with people who support your growth, and remember that every step you take toward your goals is a victory. You have the power to rebuild your life—one choice, one action, one day at a time."

Ramon Day – Rebuilding a Life

In the vibrant community of Pittsburg, California, Ramon Day's story is a shining testament to resilience, determination, and the power of transformation. Having been free for over a decade, Ramon has not only rebuilt his life but also dedicated himself to helping others do the same through his work with the Returning Citizens Association (RCA).

Today, Ramon wears many hats: a sterile processor at the VA Hospital in Sacramento, a part-time employee at Home Depot, a homeowner, a devoted husband, a father, and the Project Director of RCA. But behind this multi-faceted life lies a journey of challenges, triumphs, and a steadfast commitment to creating a better future.

The Early Years and Challenges

Ramon grew up in Pittsburg, California, surrounded by the beauty of the Bay Area. Like many young men in his community, he faced difficult circumstances that led him down a path of incarceration. However, even in the darkest moments, Ramon never gave up on the possibility of a brighter future. He used his time in prison as an opportunity to reflect, grow, and prepare for life beyond the system.

"For me, it wasn't just about surviving incarceration—it was about rebuilding my mindset and my future. I knew I wanted more for myself and my family."

The Journey to Freedom

When Ramon was released over 10 years ago, the road ahead was far from easy. Like many returning citizens, he faced barriers to employment, housing, and social reintegration. But Ramon's resilience and determination kept him moving forward.

He worked tirelessly to establish stability, taking on roles that others might overlook. His role as a sterile processor at the VA Hospital is one he takes great pride in, knowing that his work directly supports the health and well-being of veterans. His second job at Home Depot reflects his commitment to providing for his family and achieving his goals.

Ramon's journey to homeownership is another major milestone. Becoming a homeowner was not just a personal achievement but also a testament to his dedication to creating a stable and supportive environment for his family.

Family and Community: The Heart of Ramon's Life

At the core of Ramon's journey is his family. As a loving husband and father, Ramon is driven by the desire to provide a better life for his children and create a legacy of hope and opportunity.

"My family is my foundation," he says. "They've been my biggest motivators and my greatest source of strength." But Ramon's commitment extends beyond his immediate family. As the Project Director of RCA, he works tirelessly to support system-impacted individuals as they navigate the challenges of reentry. Through mentorship, advocacy, and community initiatives, Ramon has become a beacon of hope for others looking to rebuild their lives.

A Message of Hope and Resilience

Ramon's story is a powerful reminder that life after incarceration is not only possible but also full of potential. His journey highlights the importance of community, determination, and the willingness to embrace opportunities for growth.

"Freedom isn't just about being out of prison: It's about reclaiming your life, your identity, and your purpose. It's about proving to yourself and the world that you are more than your past."

As Ramon continues to build his life and help others do the same, his story inspires all who have the privilege of hearing it. He exemplifies what it means to rise above adversity and create a future full of promise and purpose.

Ramon's words to others embarking on their reentry journey: "Believe in yourself and never stop pushing forward. Surround yourself with people who support your growth, and remember that every step you take toward your goals is a victory. You have the power to rebuild your life—one choice, one action, one day at a time."

Through his work, family, and unwavering spirit, Ramon Day continues to leave a lasting impact on his community and beyond. He is a true testament to the transformative power of resilience and hope.

How empathetic are you?

Some people are keenly in tune with the emotions of others. An empath knows what other people are feeling—sometimes before they themselves do! However, too little empathy can mean being aloof and callous; too much empathy can mean ignoring your own needs. See where you fall on this empathy scale.

From Psychology Today

Using the key below, answer the questions based on how strongly you agree or disagree with the statement. 1 for strongly disagree, 5 for strongly agree.

1. I am joyful when other people feel joyful.

　　　○　　○　　○　　○　　○
　　　1　　2　　3　　4　　5
　　DISAGREE　　　　　**AGREE**

2. I don't want to hear my friend's problems.

　　　○　　○　　○　　○　　○
　　　1　　2　　3　　4　　5
　　DISAGREE　　　　　**AGREE**

3. I feel compassionate towards those who've had bad luck in life.

　　　○　　○　　○　　○　　○
　　　1　　2　　3　　4　　5
　　DISAGREE　　　　　**AGREE**

4. I get annoyed when a friend is teary.

　　　○　　○　　○　　○　　○
　　　1　　2　　3　　4　　5
　　DISAGREE　　　　　**AGREE**

5. I defend people who are treated unfairly.

　　　○　　○　　○　　○　　○
　　　1　　2　　3　　4　　5
　　DISAGREE　　　　　**AGREE**

6. I don't understand why people cry with joy.

○ ○ ○ ○ ○
1 2 3 4 5
DISAGREE   **AGREE**

7. I am patient with people and their questions.

○ ○ ○ ○ ○
1 2 3 4 5
DISAGREE   **AGREE**

8. If I read fiction, I can't get into the characters' mindset.

○ ○ ○ ○ ○
1 2 3 4 5
DISAGREE   **AGREE**

9. I try to think about the other person's feelings before giving them feedback.

○ ○ ○ ○ ○
1 2 3 4 5
DISAGREE   **AGREE**

10. In conversation with others, my mind wanders.

○ ○ ○ ○ ○
1 2 3 4 5
DISAGREE   **AGREE**

Subtract the second number from the first number to get your answer.
Use the key below to determine whether or not you have a healthy amount of empathy.

○ − ○ = ○

Add up the answers for every
odd number

Add up the answers for every
even number

Your number

😤 0-6	💖 7-15	😰 16-20
Self-Involved Your feelings and your perspective are valid and important, but remember to extend this right to others as well.	**Empath** Anyone would be lucky to call you a friend! You are in touch with your own emotions and help others feel seen and heard.	**Codependent** While having empathy for others is important, putting their emotional wellbeing over your own may be a sign to improve your self-care.

The Ripple Effect of Reentry Programs

How RCA Programs Are Changing Lives and Communities

Reentry programs are more than a lifeline for individuals returning to society after incarceration—they are catalysts for change that extend far beyond the individuals they serve. The Returning Citizens Association (RCA) has been at the forefront of this effort, creating programs that not only support returning citizens but also positively impact their families, neighborhoods, and society as a whole.

Building Stronger Families

RCA's reentry programs focus on providing participants with the tools they need to rebuild their lives, starting with their families. For many, incarceration creates emotional and physical distance from loved ones. RCA bridges that gap through mentorship, non-clinical mental health support, and workshops that emphasize communication, trust, and emotional resilience.

One participant shared, "The mentorship I received through RCA didn't just help me—it helped me reconnect with my family. I learned how to communicate better, how to be present, and how to support my loved ones." When returning citizens heal and grow, their families benefit. Children gain a parent who is more engaged, spouses find a supportive partner, and extended family members experience the ripple effect of stability and hope.

Take Nina's story, for example. As a participant in RCA's non-clinical mental health support group, Nina found the courage to take on a new role in her family. Her nephew's parents are currently incarcerated, and Nina decided to pursue full custody to provide him with a stable and loving home. She credits the support group with giving her the confidence and emotional tools to take this life-changing step. "The program helped me realize I'm stronger than I thought. It gave me the courage to stand up and take responsibility for my nephew's future," Nina shared.

Revitalizing Neighborhoods

RCA programs also have a direct impact on neighborhoods. Through initiatives like the Reentry Mentorship Program and Tapped-In Magazine, RCA provides returning citizens with opportunities to contribute meaningfully to their communities. Whether it's sharing stories that inspire others, volunteering, or mentoring youth, program participants become active, positive forces in their neighborhoods.

Communities that once viewed returning citizens with skepticism are now seeing them as assets. They bring resilience, creativity, and lived experience that can inspire and drive change.

A Broader Impact on Society

The ripple effect of RCA programs extends to society at large. By focusing on reducing recidivism, RCA helps decrease the financial and social costs of incarceration. Every individual who successfully reintegrates into society saves taxpayer dollars and reduces the burden on an already overburdened criminal justice system.

Additionally, RCA's programs challenge societal stigma around incarceration by amplifying the voices of system-impacted individuals. Initiatives like Tapped-In Magazine and the Building Resilience Summit Series showcase the strength and potential of returning citizens, shifting public perception and encouraging broader support for reentry programs.

Richard Gaines, Executive Director of RCA, explains, "Our mission isn't just about helping individuals—it's about creating a ripple effect that transforms entire communities. When we invest in returning citizens, we're investing in a stronger, more compassionate society."

Stories of Transformation

The success of RCA programs can be seen in the stories of those they've impacted:
- Jose, a mentee in the RCA Reentry Mentorship Program, reconnected with his family, found a community of positive individuals, and now mentors others navigating reentry.
- Nina, who participates in RCA's non-clinical mental health support group, gained the courage to take custody of her nephew, giving him a safe and loving home while his parents are incarcerated.
- Ramon, an RCA participant, found healing through the non-clinical mental health support group after years of struggling with the grief of losing his son in a tragic car accident. "I never thought I could talk about it without breaking down," Ramon shared. "But through the support group, I've been able to share my story, find healing, and even help others who are dealing with their own pain."

These stories highlight the real, measurable impact of RCA's work and underscore the importance of continued support for reentry initiatives.

The Path Forward

The ripple effect of RCA programs is undeniable, but there is still much work to be done. RCA is committed to expanding its reach, building partnerships, and continuing to advocate for policies that support returning citizens.

"We believe in the power of second chances. When we support individuals in their reentry journey, we're not just changing their lives—we're changing the world around them."

- Richard Gaines, RCA Executive Director

Reuniting Families
after incarceration

The Story of Richard & Andrea Gaines

When Richard Gaines walked out of the California Department of Corrections and Rehabilitation (CDCR) after 24 years of incarceration, he wasn't just stepping into freedom—he was stepping into the unknown. For years, incarceration had kept him apart from his family, creating both emotional and physical distance. His release was the start of a new journey—reconnecting with his loved ones and rebuilding the trust that had been lost over time.

This is not just Richard's story—it is the story of countless justice-impacted individuals striving to mend fractured relationships and reclaim their roles within their families.

"Seeing my husband walk through that door was like a dream come true. It wasn't easy—we had to learn to communicate all over again. But every small step we took brought us closer."

The Emotional Challenges of Reuniting

Reuniting with loved ones after incarceration can be both exciting and challenging. For Richard, the first hug from his children was a moment of pure joy, but it also came with an undercurrent of uncertainty. "I didn't know how to begin again," Richard recalls. "There was so much I wanted to say, but I also didn't want to overwhelm them. I wasn't the same person who went in, and they weren't the same people I left behind." The emotional toll of incarceration affects both the incarcerated individual and their family. Years of separation can create feelings of resentment, guilt, and mistrust. For Richard, the hardest part was addressing the pain his absence had caused, especially with his family, who had taken on responsibilities in his absence.

The Rewards of Reconnection

Despite the challenges, the rewards of reuniting are profound. Richard's wife, Andrea, shares her perspective: "Seeing my husband walk through that door was like a dream come true. It wasn't easy—we had to learn to communicate all over again. But every small step we took brought us closer." For Richard, moments like birthdays or cooking dinner with his wife became milestones of healing. These everyday activities helped create a new normal, allowing the family to rebuild their bond one moment at a time.

Expert Advice on Navigating Family Dynamics

We spoke with wife of Richard Gaines, Andrea Gaines, who spent 10 years supporting him while he was incarcerated, to understand the complexities of this process. The two have been together for 15 plus years.

"Reuniting families after incarceration is about managing expectations," Andrea explains. "Both sides need time and patience. It's not just about picking up where you left off; it's about creating something new together." Andrea shares the following tips:

Start Slow: Don't rush the process. Begin with open, honest conversations, and allow time to rebuild trust.
Acknowledge the Past: Avoid sweeping unresolved issues under the rug.
Acknowledge mistakes, express remorse, and focus on growth.
Set Boundaries: Rebuilding relationships doesn't mean forfeiting personal boundaries.
Clearly communicate needs and limits.
Seek Professional Support: Family counseling or support groups can provide a
neutral space for communication and healing.

See page 52 for a list of helpful resources.

Soft Skills for Success

Thriving in Work and Life through Communication, Time Management, and Teamwork

Soft skills—often referred to as "people skills"—are as essential as technical expertise when navigating the demands of work and life. These intangible but highly valuable skills improve how you connect with others, manage your time, and function within a team. Whether you're stepping into a new role, navigating a career change, or rebuilding your life after reentry, soft skills can serve as a cornerstone for success and personal growth.

1. Communication: The Key to Understanding

Strong communication skills are fundamental to building meaningful relationships and preventing misunderstandings. They enable you to express your thoughts clearly, actively engage with others, and foster mutual understanding.

- **Active Listening:** Communication is a two-way street. Pay close attention to what others are saying, ask clarifying questions when needed, and paraphrase their words to confirm understanding. This shows respect and ensures effective dialogue.
- **Non-Verbal Communication:** Actions often speak louder than words. Maintain appropriate eye contact, use open gestures, and align your tone and posture with your message. Awareness of non-verbal cues also helps you gauge others' feelings and reactions.
- **Practice Empathy:** Understanding others' perspectives requires stepping into their shoes. Empathy strengthens relationships and builds trust, even in difficult situations.

Pro Tip: Role-playing exercises and communication workshops can provide practical opportunities to improve both verbal and non-verbal communication skills.

2. Time Management: Making the Most of Every Day

Time is your most finite and valuable resource. Mastering time management is essential for achieving your goals without unnecessary stress.

- **Set Priorities:** Not all tasks are created equal. Use tools like the Eisenhower Matrix to separate urgent and important tasks from less critical ones.
- **Break Tasks into Steps:** Overwhelmed by a big project? Divide it into smaller, more manageable pieces, and tackle them one at a time.
- **Use Tools:** Digital tools like Google Calendar, Trello, and Asana can help you track deadlines, set reminders, and stay organized.
- **Avoid Procrastination:** Identify distractions and create a focused work environment. The Pomodoro Technique—working in focused intervals with breaks—can boost productivity.

Pro Tip: Reflect on your daily achievements and adjust your plans as needed. Consistently reviewing your progress helps you refine your time management strategies.

3. Teamwork: Collaboration for Success

In today's collaborative environments, teamwork is a critical ingredient for achieving shared goals. Effective teamwork is about building relationships, adapting to dynamics, and contributing meaningfully to collective efforts.

- **Be Reliable:** Consistency builds trust. Complete tasks on time, meet commitments, and communicate openly when challenges arise.
- **Adapt to Different Roles:** Flexibility is key. Whether you're leading a project, supporting a colleague, or brain storming ideas, embrace the role that best serves your team.
- **Resolve Conflicts Gracefully:** Disagreements are natural, but they don't have to derail progress. Address conflicts calmly, listen actively, and work toward mutually beneficial solutions.
- **Celebrate Wins:** Recognizing team accomplishments fosters morale and strengthens group cohesion. A simple "thank you" or acknowledgment of others' efforts can go a long way.

Pro Tip: Participate in team-building activities or volunteer projects to hone your collaborative skills in low-pressure environments.

Building Soft Skills: A Lifelong Process

Soft skills are not static; they evolve with practice and experience. For ongoing development:

- **Seek Feedback:** Constructive feedback from trusted colleagues, mentors, or friends can offer valuable insights into areas for improvement.
- **Invest in Learning:** Enroll in workshops, online courses, or mentorship programs that focus on communication, leadership, and time management.
- **Practice Daily:** Opportunities to refine soft skills are all around you—whether it's through resolving a personal conflict, managing a household schedule, or participating in a community project.

Thriving Beyond the Workplace

Soft skills are not just career assets; they enrich your personal life, strengthen relationships, and enhance your contributions to the community. By mastering these skills, you're paving the way for a brighter, more resilient future. Whether you're communicating effectively with a friend, managing your time to achieve personal goals, or collaborating on a community initiative, soft skills empower you to thrive in every aspect of life.

Visual Stories of Resilience

By Lacey Kilgrove, Founder of Curated By the Collective

I don't believe in coincidences. I met Richard and Andrea Gaines while I was on a summer road trip in New Mexico at Santuario de Chimayo in 2023. We began talking and realized our goals were aligned; they were starting the Returning Citizens Association and I was starting Curated By The Collective. Our relationship grew from there as they welcomed me into their RCA family and invited me to speak at the first Building Resilience Summit Series later that year. While I do not consider myself a system-impacted person, I do believe that the dysfunctional criminal justice system in America hurts us all. It's an honor to contribute to their heroic efforts by helping with creative needs for the RCA, Tapped-In Magazine being one of my favorites!

Meeting Jay and Karen

I was wandering around Governor's Island in New York City one day when I stumbled upon an exhibition from Escaping Time and met Jay Darden and Karen Thomas. Seeing all of the artwork displayed on the walls, I was immediately inspired to inquire about the artists and tell them about the amazing work RCA was doing. It seemed like the Universe was guiding me to the right people at the right time to make meaningful connections that had the potential to make a much larger impact than I could have ever imagined.

Learning about the process of creating artwork with materials found in prison was eye-opening, and I gained a new understanding of how freeing art can truly be. The name "Escaping Time" took on a new meaning for me as both Jay and Karen explained how much creating art saved their lives while incarcerated. "I taught myself how to paint by going to the library and practicing as often as I could" Jay explained *(pictured to the left with his artwork.)* He began curating and organizing the exhibitions for the nonprofit and manages the entire process of receiving, storing, displaying, and selling artwork for people who are still incarcerated. "It's important to me that each person receives compensation for their artwork" he noted.

One particular piece make such a profound impact on me, I had to purchase it immediately *(pictured to the left.)* I was moved to tears hearing Karen share that this particular series of windows was created for the window-less room she was kept in for years. "My first piece showed the image of a woman on the edge of a bed with a tiny sliver of light coming through" she told me. "One day a man walked into the gallery and asked if that's what it was really like, and I said it was" she went on to explain. "Little did I know, the man ended up being an architect for New York state prisons and was inspired to change the design of the cells based on my artwork."

The following pages showcase artwork from incarcerated people and can be purchased by visiting **escapingtime.org**. I hope you are just as inspired as I was. ⭐

Not Guilty by **Jairo Pastoressa** | **$200**

"Toocan" & Sam by David Nelson | $75

Bamboo by Chad Goetsch | $180

Helping Grandma by Karen Thomas | $200

Woman in Green Print by Jay Darden | $15

Dreaming by Randy Venzie | $200

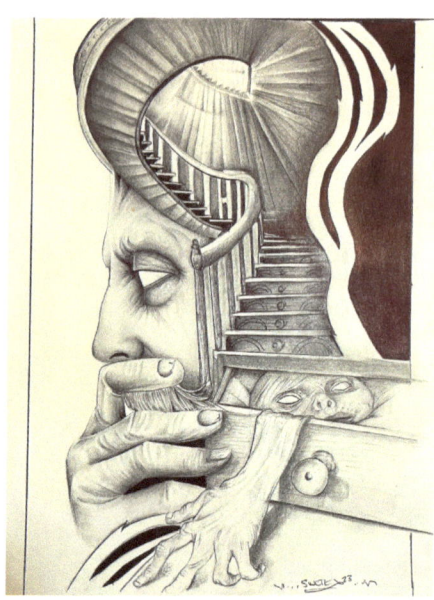

Staircase #2 by Josh Swetky | $300

Dragon by Andrae Nelson | $100

Fancy Dancer by Michael Tenneson | $400

Skull Kiss by Chad A. Galvan | $100

Panther isla estuarte pequeña
by Scott Arends | $40

Various Butterfly Sculptures
by Mark Springer | $25

As The Sun Awoke!
by David Lange | $80

Mexican Streetscape by James Cranfill | $325

Into The Distance by Soden | $150

Scan the QR code to visit escapingtime.org to view all of the artwork available for purchase.

Email info@escapingtime.org to submit artwork for a loved one who is currently incarcerated, or send the pieces directly to Escaping Time, P.O. BOX 2676, Plainfield, NJ 07060.

A ZINE DESIGNED TO EDUCATE ALLIES & EMPOWER SYSTEM-IMPACTED ARTISTS

Art + Agency

The Art + Agency zine includes guiding principles for organizations/institutions and a guide for artists in carceral spaces that covers the fundamentals of safely marketing and publishing their work, advice about pricing their work, and tips for self-advocacy. This zine is a reference point for building ethical standards to which entities and individuals hold themselves accountable when exhibiting, selling, and/or publishing creative work by artists impacted by the criminal legal system.

The facilitation process was led by Kamisha Thomas and Aimee Wissman, co-founders of the Returning Artists Guild, and Page Dukes (Mourning Our Losses), with the insight of a working group consisting of seven artists who are incarcerated across the country. Learn more about the Justice Arts Coalition in the back of our magazine.

Educating Allies and
Empowering Artists
in Carceral Spaces

1

About Art + Agency:
The conversation began during a roundtable at Justice Arts Coalition's (JAC) 2021 National Convening Art for a New Future. Since then, the Art + Agency team was formed and has been diligently working to keep the dialogue going. Art + Agency centers the experiences and leadership of artists with lived experience of incarceration in developing guiding principles intended to become the standard to which organizations, institutions, and individuals that exhibit, sell, and/or publish creative work by system-impacted individuals hold themselves accountable.

The facilitation of this process has been led by JAC partners Kamisha Thomas and Aimee Wissman, Co-Founders of the Returning Artists Guild (RAG) and Page Dukes of Mourning Our Losses. Over the past six months, they have been in regular correspondence with a working group of artists who are or have been incarcerated, collecting the artists' feedback through a series of surveys and interviews. Each Working Group member has had opportunities to both share their own experiences and reflect on the experiences shared by their colleagues. The members of the Working Group are:

Carole Alden (UT)
Brett Gonzalez (TX)
Spoon Jackson (CA)
EJ Joyner (GA)
William B. Livingston III (OK)
Kenneth Reams (AR)
Carla Joan Simmons (GA)

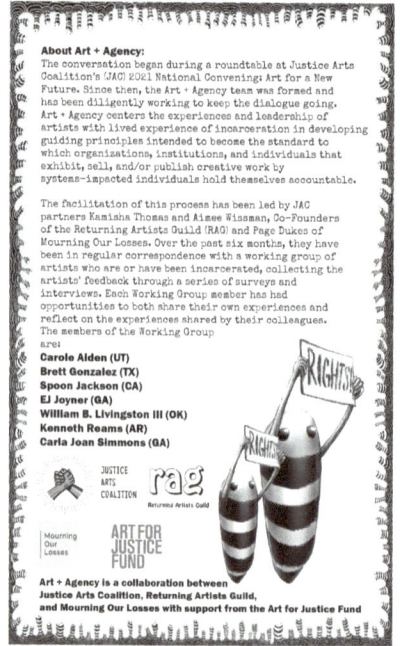

Art + Agency is a collaboration between Justice Arts Coalition, Returning Artists Guild, and Mourning Our Losses with support from the Art for Justice Fund

2

Scan the QR code to learn more about the project and to download a free copy of the full zine.

ARTISTS' CREDO

I have the right to find and create opportunities to support my own art practice, to partner with staff/volunteers who can be partnered with, and to support the development of other artists inside.

I have the right to assert my creativity, ingenuity, and ability to teach myself, to discover new ideas, to practice my craft, and to monetize my work in the ways that I choose.

I have the right to control my own narrative, including how I am referenced and what parts of my story are public vs. private.

Artists don't work for free, and I have the right to ask questions about compensation, including:

- **What exactly am I being compensated for?** For my time and labor? For a project? For a piece, object, or outcome?

- **How am I being paid?** Money on my books, supplies, boxes/in-kind support, money sent to a family member or trusted outside ally?

- **When will I receive the payment?**

- **Do you have a contract?** Can I create a contract for us?

- **What additional costs do I have?** Shipping, communication, etc. Those should be covered expenses.

- **Can you agree to document my work and share it with me through photos, JPAY, etc.?**

- **Can you agree to a plan for how and when we will communicate?**

I have the right to leave or stop any project at any time. The nature of my confinement limits my access to communication and information, disrupts my daily routines, and is constantly changing, therefore, I have the right to walk away from any project with or without further explanation.

An essence examined

by a bitterness handed to me

over and over again

 brushed off

and rebuked by love

over and over again

see I refuse to let this system win

and though my head is blooded

and my soul is bruised

My spirit enlarges

like a muscle infused

Because every hard thing is the thing it needs to use

to become what it must be

a holy essence come true

How Malcolm and Martin

And Huey were made

how the praying ladies prayed

And the children ceased to play

When essence demanded

a time to disobey

The legacy of essence

Eternally continues

The resilience and the reason

for which the seasons bear meaning

We rise and we fall and then rise once again,

We are essence, we are spirit

We are water,

 we are fire,

 we are earth

and we are wind

– Joshua Stroman

Joshua is a Harvard Divinity School graduate and criminal justice reform advocate. He is currently serving a sentence at San Quentin's Rehabilitation Center and is scheduled for release in 2025.

Excerpt from "These Songs Remind Me"

We are the children

that used to be the future.

the dried brooks in a crook's eyes,

absorbed by that oblivious sponge

inside the ordinary inertia

of being human.

Dreams that live and die

in a wet abyss

with broken fingers

at the end

of clenched fists.

This is the social tsunami

individuals

in strangled, strychnine

paradigms

playing their instruments

and singing songs

about the way we were,

and always will be.

- Ezekiel Caligiuri

A Teacher's Perspective

An Excerpt from *Teaching In The Dark: The Promise and Pedagogy of Creative Writing in Prison*

Appleman teaching a college-level writing class at a high-security men's correctional facility.

(2013) English Journal - National Council of Teachers of English

What does it mean to teach language and literature to these incarcerated students? How far will our literacy pedagogies travel? Will they travel to this darkest of places? What are the inherent tensions in promoting freedom of self-expression to the incarcerated when even their bathroom and shower habits are regulated? Does creative writing have any potential to promote correctional goals of restorative justice? These are the questions I asked myself as I prepared to teach a college-level creative writing class at a high-security men's correctional facility.

Language arts teachers from elementary school to college embrace creative writing as a useful way to unlock creative potential, to foster students' love of language and to offer a powerful outlet for self-expression. Within the teaching profession, the capacity of creative opportunity to liberate minds and hearts goes largely unchallenged. Rarely has this claim been tested, though, in the most restricted of educational settings: penitentiaries.

I attempted to create a learning environment that was as much like an ordinary class as possible in terms of pedagogical approaches, assignments, and class structure, although the presence of incarceration and surveillance was ubiquitous. In addition to the humanizing effects of the creative process, the anthology itself has notable significance for the authors. Both the publication of their work and the presentation of their reading act as a kind of liberation. Through their words, they become present in the free world, or as one incarcerated writer put it, *"I write because I cannot fly."*

"Both the publication of their work and the presentation of their reading act as a kind of liberation."

If we choose to preserve the lives of human beings who commit serious crimes, we must have some interest in helping them preserve their humanity. And, if recent statistics can be believed, the more education they receive in prison, the less likely they are to re-offend. So for a couple of hours a week anyway, these men are more than inmates: they are students, poets, interpreters, critics, and writers.

Deborah Appleman is the Hollis L. Caswell Professor of educational studies at Carleton College. Professor Appleman's recent research has focused on teaching college-level language a literature courses, and creative writing courses at the Minnesota Correctional Facility-Stillwater and the Minnesota Correctional Facility-Faribault for incarcerated men who are interested in pursuing post-secondary education.

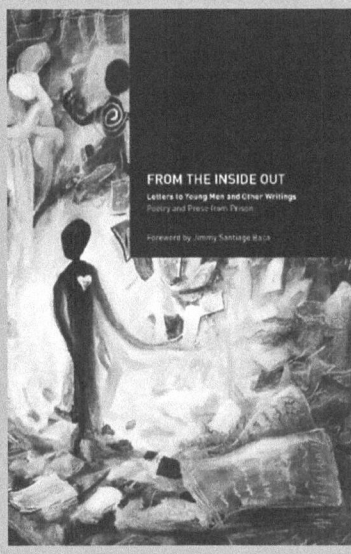

From the Inside Out: Letters to Young Men and Other Writings is a collection of art and writings from Appleman's students. All proceeds will be forwarded to the Restorative Justice Committee.

A Certain Kind

It's the sounds that lull you: the bells as a training device for animals, jingling of keys, an ever presence of authority, a constant murmur of voices until suddenly it stops. I grab the panel of steel bars and begin to close my own door, sliding on a track with the momentum of a roller coaster before the slam echoes in my core. These are the sounds that sink to silence leading you to believe this is an option you chose. I didn't have to fight anyone today, I probably won't fight tomorrow-but tonight, like every night, I'll fight the idea that I belong here, in this cage.

I think of all the men around me, with experience lying dormant under the soot of poor decisions. I know not many are scribbling in notebooks. I understand that when everything you've built is lost to a moment of impulse it is dangerous to believe that anything you craft is safe from your fire. It is a hard sell to convince a guy to start over and build on the shifty prison sands of an hourglass continually shaken. It's natural to focus on distraction and want to simply endure a prison sentence. It's sad to think that most of these stories, the ones truly worth telling, will perish in the dignity found in forgetting. Destruction begets destruction and prison kills your spirit; but creativity can resuscitate the soul. Unfortunately writing is not for everyone.

For a small number of men at Stillwater prison, it's the practice to which we've devoted our lives. I wish I could tell you how the Stillwater Writers' Collective is a band of brothers united and empowered by our efforts to prove how literature can change the prison culture.

We are responsible for atrocious acts and this is no small thing to consider. It's protocol for people to want to take us for who we are today and shun the past moral barriers we have breached; but to deny these realities is to live in denial of the deepest darkest impulses that linger at the primal bedrock of the human condition.

The problem lies in our inability to endure such contradicting emotions while holding people accountable. What do we do when a human being strays from the boundaries we set for humankind and how do we bring them back into the fold of humanity- once we have caged them? One way is writing.

Writing is the epitome of self-rehabilitation. There are no certificates for a base file, no credits for a degree to show at the end of an investment. A simple work represents years of sweat and tears and might be submitted for rejection time and time again. But the writer emerges from that work with a new understanding.

This is the creative life what Oscar Wilde called the long lovely suicide. If prison is a trapdoor at rock bottom, then writing is the mortar in between the bricks you must pry in order to dig your way out.

The truth of the matter is that writing is hard. It takes a certain kind of crazed obsession no matter what your environment. If everyone has a story to tell, why aren't some ever told? How many of us have compromised the craft for family or friends, to raise children or teach others?

Writing requires a balance of living a life worth writing about and doing the work. In the process you are changed and the moment of epiphany comes when you begin to read your life as a writer. Everything around you becomes part of the craft. You see the plot in the narratives unfolding in real time. You can realize relationships are complex characters making the decisions you may or may not agree with. People couldn't script some of the shit you go through, so you mold it as a lesson to be learned.

It takes a certain kind of will to begin to pick up shattered pieces of a life laid before us. It takes a certain kind of courage to mourn what was broken and confront the value of that which was lost by our hand. It takes a certain kind of creativity to craft those broken shards through audacity and hope, into something that pays respect to the past yet bears a responsibility to a future. And it takes a certain kind of benevolence to invest in the fallen--a complex compassion that can forgive without forgetting, that believes that moving on doesn't absolve accountability.

In my cramped cell, where I eat, work and sleep mere feet from a toilet, I sit and ponder how to use this fleeting moment—what to say to you lightning bugs who have wandered into our glass jars. Through continued support, convicts can come home better people; but the formula is flawed. Enduring a retributive prison sentence does little to honor our victims. It's in taking hold of our story that we can still turn it around for a greater good. Only in finding a form of success can we get to a point where we can help others. We must combat that insurmountable debt-a debt we owe not to society, but to humanity.

Don't wait until we are released to invest in us. Everyone needs to be heard in order to know the value of their voice. The dignity of the damned must be redeemed. Thank you for all you have already done and all you are willing to do. Go tell your friends, family, co-workers, politicians, anyone who will listen that we exist—for better or worse. And we will continue to grow and refine our voice until it is amplified to the explosive degree that blows a hole in the wall. Not for us to escape, but for society to see inside and explore ideas of justice in a place we are all taught to fear and dismiss.

- C. Fausto Cabrera

Cabrera was one of Professor Appleman's students while incarcerated and has recently been released.

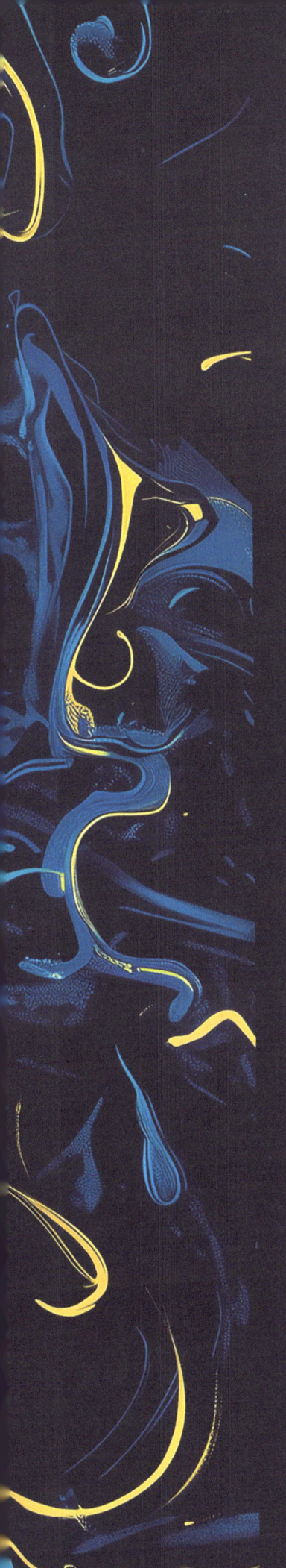

SIGNS OF A PANIC ATTACK

NUMBNESS

SHORTNESS OF BREATH

TREMBLING

RAPID HEARTBEAT

DIZZINESS

SWEATING

FEAR OF DEATH

CHEST PAIN

STEPS TO CALM DOWN

1. Take a few deep breaths

2. Tell yourself you're safe

Our bodies are responding to a traumatic memory. Come back to the present moment by naming five things you can see, four things you can hear, three things you can smell, two things you can feel, and one thing you can taste.

3. Try progressive muscle relaxation

Close your eyes and feel the weight of your body on your seat. Focus your awareness on your toes and feel them relax. Visualize a healing light at each body part until you've made it all the way up to the crown of your head.

4. Visualize a peaceful place

5. Move & splash cold water on yourself

The Future of Reentry

Insights from experts in criminal justice reform, education, and mental health on what lies ahead

The journey of reentry is complex, filled with challenges but also opportunities for transformation. For this special feature, Tapped-In Magazine brings together four incredible voices with lived experience—Richard Gaines, Anthony Partee, Denise Coleman, and Marcus Sanders—to share their insights on the future of reentry. With expertise in criminal justice reform, education, and mental health, these leaders reflect on the progress made and what lies ahead for system-impacted individuals.

The State of Reentry Today

What do you see as the biggest challenges facing people reentering society today?

Richard Gaines (Criminal Justice Advocate):
The stigma attached to incarceration remains one of the biggest barriers. Employers, landlords, and even communities often define system-impacted individuals by their past mistakes rather than their potential. This stigma not only limits opportunities but also reinforces cycles of poverty and recidivism. We need to push for policies that support second chances and educate society about the value of lived experience.

Denise Coleman (Mental Health Practitioner):
Mental health is another critical issue. Many people exiting incarceration face untreated trauma, depression, or anxiety. Without proper support, these challenges can spiral, making it harder to reintegrate. Access to non-clinical peer support, therapy, and resources must be prioritized as part of the reentry process.

Anthony Partee (Community Organizer and Financial Coach):
I'd say access to education and job training is a massive hurdle. While incarcerated, many people don't get the skills they need to compete in today's workforce. When they're released, they're expected to rebuild their lives without the tools to do so. We have to rethink how we approach education during incarceration and provide stronger transitional programs.

Marcus Sanders (Youth Mentor and Educator):
Reentry doesn't just affect the individual—it impacts families and entire communities. The lack of support for families of the incarcerated is a major issue. When we talk about reentry, we have to consider the ripple effect. Providing resources to families is just as important as supporting those directly impacted.

Innovative Solutions for the Future
What innovations or strategies do you think can transform the reentry process?

R: The rise of technology in reentry programs is promising. For example, virtual mentorship platforms can connect system-impacted individuals with mentors from anywhere in the world. This can help fill gaps in areas where in-person resources are limited.

D: Trauma-informed care is essential. We need to build programs that address the underlying trauma many people carry. Peer-led mental health support groups, like those offered by the Returning Citizens Association, are a great example of how we can create safe spaces for healing and growth.

A: We need to focus on second-chance hiring initiatives. Employers have a huge role to play in reentry. By creating pathways for system-impacted individuals to access stable jobs, we reduce recidivism and help people regain dignity. Partnering with businesses to provide skills training and internships can make a significant difference.

M: Community-based education is the future. Programs that involve families, schools, and local organizations can help individuals transition more smoothly. For instance, youth mentorship programs can reduce the intergenerational impact of incarceration by providing young people with positive role models and support.

Hopes for the Future
What's your vision for the future of reentry?

R: I want to see a world where reentry is not just a process but a transformation. We need to build systems that focus on healing, opportunity, and equity. Everyone deserves a second chance, and it's up to us to create a society that believes in that.

D: My hope is that mental health support becomes a standard part of reentry programs. By addressing emotional and psychological needs, we can help people build stronger foundations for their new lives.

A: I envision a future where education is accessible to everyone, regardless of their circumstances. Whether it's earning a GED, a trade certification, or a college degree, education should be the bridge to a better life.

M: My dream is for communities to take an active role in reentry. When we invest in people, not just policies, we create a network of support that ensures long-term success.

"Reentry isn't the end of a journey— it's the beginning of something new."

– Richard Gaines

My Journey Towards Healthy Relationships

By Jose Ramirez, RCA Mentor and Speaker

To build healthy relationships, we must first cultivate health within ourselves. This requires understanding our emotions, recognizing our triggers, and learning to differentiate between feelings and logic. When we achieve this self-awareness, it becomes easier to respond thoughtfully to others rather than react impulsively. Healthy relationships thrive on accountability, mutual respect, and the ability to agree to disagree without resentment. Before I became a Christian, my relationships were damaged by my selfishness, mistrust, and inability to value others genuinely. My past actions hurt many, including my family. I focused on my needs, burning bridges and neglecting the people closest to me. The turning point came after my arrest for murder, which left me feeling as though I had lost everything, including my relationship with my children.

In my despair, I turned to God. Thirty days after my arrest, I gave my life to Him, seeking forgiveness and guidance. Through prayer and studying the Bible, I began to align my values with God's principles. I learned that God accepts us as we are, hates our sins but not us, and offers unconditional love. This realization transformed me. I began to practice trust, forgiveness, and love in my relationships, starting with my mom.

Forgiveness as a Cornerstone

As I rebuilt my relationship with my mom, I asked for her forgiveness for the shame and hurt I caused. She forgave me without hesitation. This moment taught me that forgiveness is key to mending broken relationships. It allows us to move forward without resentment, building trust and opening the door to honest communication.

Practicing Vulnerability and Empathy

I once viewed vulnerability as weakness, but I've learned it is a strength. Being vulnerable allows us to express our true selves and fosters deeper connections. When I shared my regrets with my daughter, asking for her forgiveness, it created a foundation for rebuilding our relationship. Empathy, too, has been transformative. It's not about pity but about understanding and sharing another person's feelings.

One of my mentors, Pastor Mel, taught me the power of empathy. He visited me in jail, listened without judgment, and showed me that love and understanding can exist even in the darkest circumstances. His example inspired me to practice empathy in all my relationships, which has brought healing and growth.

Unconditional Love in Action

Unconditional love, as exemplified by Jesus Christ, has become my guiding principle. This love requires patience, acceptance, and a willingness to endure hardships for the sake of others. It's not about what we can gain but about giving freely, even when it's difficult. With my children, I've faced challenges. My daughter, now 13, is slowly rebuilding trust with me, though she still has doubts. My son, 11, has not yet been open to reconnecting. Despite this, I remain committed to loving them unconditionally, respecting their feelings, and continuing to show up for them.

A Transformative Mentorship Journey

My transformation gained momentum when I joined the Returning Citizens Association (RCA)'s Mentorship Program as a mentee. Calling into the program from prison, I connected with my mentor, Ricky Gaines, who guided me with patience, empathy, and wisdom. Ricky's mentorship helped me reflect on my values, understand my emotions, and begin the process of healing my relationships with my children, family, and, most importantly, myself. The program gave me tools and a supportive community that empowered me to rebuild my life. By the time I completed the mentorship program, I had developed a new perspective on relationships and resilience. This foundation became critical as I prepared for my release on August 31, 2024.

Rebuilding and Giving Back

Upon my release, I embraced the opportunity to give back to the RCA community by becoming a mentor. Today, I help other system-impacted individuals navigate the challenges of reentry and personal growth. Sharing my experiences with others has been deeply rewarding and has reinforced my commitment to fostering healthy relationships, both personally and professionally. One of my proudest moments as a mentor was speaking at RCA's Building Resilience Summit Series in San Francisco on December 13, 2024. Standing before a crowd of community members, I shared my journey of transformation and the role RCA played in helping me rebuild my life.

The Ingredients of Healthy Relationships

Through my journey, I've identified key elements for maintaining healthy relationships:

Trust: Built through honesty and consistency.
Forgiveness: Frees us from grudges and enables growth.
Effective Communication: Requires active listening, understanding, and clarity.
Empathy: Strengthens connections by allowing us to share others' feelings.
Vulnerability: Encourages authenticity and fosters deeper bonds.
Unconditional Love: Anchors relationships in selflessness and commitment.
Positivity: Keeps relationships uplifting and forward-focused.

Learning and Growing

I've learned that relationships require continual effort, patience, and self-awareness. Not every relationship will work out, and that's okay. Sometimes, choosing your health over maintaining a toxic connection is necessary. As I prepare to return home in 2024, I carry these lessons with me. I'm committed to restoring and nurturing my relationships with my children, family, and others in my life. Healthy relationships are not perfect—they are built on understanding, acceptance, and mutual respect, even in the face of challenges.

If you're working to build healthier relationships, I encourage you to start with self-awareness, forgiveness, and a commitment to unconditional love. Remember, it's not about perfection—it's about progress.

Resource Directory

This comprehensive directory is designed to connect system-impacted individuals and those currently incarcerated with essential services and support. Whether planning for reentry or navigating life after release, these organizations provide employment opportunities, housing, legal aid, mental health support, and financial literacy resources.

Second-Chance Employers

The Doe Fund
Job training, transitional work, and permanent employment opportunities.
(212) 690-6480 | info@doe.org
345 E 102nd St #305, New York NY 10029

Jail to Jobs
Paid internships, mentorship, and job placement for justice-impacted youth.
(512) 407-9020 | 737.234.5627
office@jailtojobs.com
PO Box 2737 Cedar Park, TX 78630

Dave's Killer Bread
Employment assistance and resources for formerly incarcerated individuals.
5209 SE International Way, Milwaukie, OR 97222

Transitional Housing Programs

Oxford House, Inc.
Affordable, peer-managed sober housing.
1010 Wayne Avenue, Suite 300
Silver Spring, MD 20910
www.oxfordhouse.org

Building Opportunities for Self-Sufficiency (BOSS)
Offers transitional housing, mentorship, and reentry support services.

1918 University Ave, Suite 2A
Berkeley, CA 94704 | info@self-sufficiency.org
(510) 649-1930

Hope Hall
Faith-based transitional housing for justice-impacted individuals.
(312) 564-2373 | info@voail.org
1919 Main Street, Melrose, IL 60160
www.voans.org/locations/hope-hall/

Legal Aid Services

Equal Justice Initiative (EJI)
Legal advocacy for systemic injustice and reentry support.
www.eji.org
122 Commerce Street
Montgomery, AL 36104
(334) 269-1803

Root & Rebound
Reentry legal education and support.
(510) 279-4662 | info@rootandrebound.org
PO Box 118
201 13th St OFC
Oakland, CA 9461228

Legal Aid Society
Legal support for housing, employment, and family law for returning citizens.
(212) 577-3300

Bronx Neighborhood Office
(718) 991-4758
260 E. 161st Street
Bronx, New York 10451

Mental Health Support

Returning Citizens Association (RCA)
*Peer support groups, mentorship,
and resilience classes.*
(510) 872-2832
rca@returningcitizensassoc.org
490 Lake Park Ave #10552, Oakland, CA 94610

National Alliance on Mental Illness (NAMI)
*Free mental health resources, support groups,
and crisis lines.*
(703) 524-7600
4301 Wilson Blvd., Suite 300
Arlington, VA 22203

Prison Mindfulness Institute
*Mindfulness training for incarcerated individuals
and returning citizens.*
PO Box 206, South Deerfield, MA 01373

Employment Readiness Programs

Defy Ventures
*Entrepreneurship training and financial literacy
for returning citizens.*
5 Penn Plaza, 19th Floor, New York, Ny 10001

Operation HOPE
*Financial literacy education, credit counseling,
and small business support. Credit & Money
Management.*
HOPE Inside U.S. Bank
1970 Franklin Street, Oakland, CA 94612

America Works
*Workforce development and employment
placement for system-impacted individuals.*
(415) 552-9675 | info@americaworks.com
275 5th Street, Suite 307
San Francisco, CA 94103

For Incarcerated Individuals
*Write to these organizations for guidance,
resources, and support while planning your reentry:*

Returning Citizens Association (RCA)
(510) 872-2832 | rca@returningcitizensassoc.org
490 Lake Park Ave #10552, Oakland, CA 94610

Prison Fellowship
P.O. Box 1550, Merrifield, VA 22116-1550

Prison Book Program
c/o Lucy Parsons Bookstore
1306 Hancock Street, Suite 100
Quincy, MA 02169
info@prisonbookprogram.org

Root & Rebound
Reentry legal education and support.
(510) 279-4662 | info@rootandrebound.org
PO Box 118
201 13th St OFC
Oakland, CA 9461228

Resources for Families

**National Resource Center on Children and Families
of the Incarcerated**
*Offers resources and support for families
navigating reunification.*
nrccfi.camden.rutgers.edu

Returning Citizens Association (RCA)
*Provides mentorship, workshops, and non-clinical
support for families impacted by incarceration.*
www.returningcitizensassoc.org

The National Reentry Resource Center
*Provides tools and guidance for individuals and
families during the reentry process.*
csgjusticecenter.org/nrrc

RCA RE-ENTRY MENTORSHIP PROGRAM

MONTH 1
PROGRAM LAUNCH

Week 1: Application forms are made available online and distributed to prisons, correctional facilities and community organizations.

Weeks 2-4: RCA actively promotes the program, encourages participation and collects applications from individuals still incarcerated and seeking reintegration opportunities.

MONTH 2
REVIEW & SELECTION

Weeks 1-2: RCA staff conducts telephone interviews and assessments with each applicant to identify motivated individuals who will benefit most from the program.

Weeks 3-4: Based on the assessment results, RCA carefully matches each participant with a suitable mentor who has successfully reintegrated into society. Pairs are established.

MONTHS 3 - 6
SKILL-BUILDING

Weeks 1-4: Participants engage in weekly phone sessions with their mentors to develop personalized reentry plans, set achievable goals, and identify resources & strategies for successful reintegration.

Weeks 5-12: RCA organizes weekly phone-based workshops, job readiness training and networking events to enhance participants' employability, soft skills and economic independence.

MONTHS 7 - 9
SUPPORT NETWORK

Weeks 1-12: Participants join phone-based group sessions facilitated by RCA staff, offering a supportive network of peers and professionals. The sessions foster camaraderie & ongoing support that allow experiences to be shared. Participants are encouraged to practice their soft skills and further develop their emotional intelligence.

MONTHS 10 - 12
GRADUATION

Weeks 1-2: RCA collects feedback from mentors, mentees and other stakeholders to evaluate the program's effectiveness & identify areas for improvement.

Weeks 3-4: RCA provides additional resources and support for reentry.

Week 5: The program concludes with a graduation ceremony celebrating participants' growth and achievements.

Ready to Join? Take these steps to become a mentee

1 APPLICATION
Your journey to empowerment starts here! Fill out the application from wherever you are.

2 TELEPHONE INTERVIEW
Get ready to share your story and talk with an RCA member about your goals & challenges.

3 MEET YOUR MENTOR
Get paired with a mentor who will schedule regular sessions to help you achieve your unique goals.

4 CREATE YOUR PLAN
With your mentor's guidance, set achievable goals, identify resources and conquer challenges.

5 DEVELOP YOUR SKILLS
Gain access to educational resources, skill-building workshops and job readiness training.

6 ACTIVE PARTICIPATION
Participate in the weekly sessions and take advantage of the support network. Engage in all program components.

7 PROGRAM EVALUATION
Your journey matters! Provide your honest feedback on the program so we can continue to make improvements.

Application Form - RCA Reentry Mentorship Program

Please fill out this application form to be considered for the RCA Reentry Mentorship Program. *All information provided will be treated with the utmost confidentiality.*

Full Name: _____   Incarceration Facility Name: _____

Date of Birth: _____   Expected Release Date: _____

Gender: _____   Phone Number (Correctional Facility): _____

Address: _____   Contact Information: _____

City: _____   _____

State: _____

Zip Code: _____

Phone Number (Alternate if available): _____

Background Information:

What are your goals and aspirations upon release?

What do you hope to achieve through the mentorship program?

Do you have any specific challenges you anticipate during reentry?

What skills or interests do you have that you would like to develop or explore further?

Do you have any existing support systems (family, friends, etc.) to assist you during reentry?

(Optional) Please provide the names and contact information of up to two references who can speak about your character and potential for reintegration.

Is there any other information you would like us to consider during the application process?

By submitting this application, you confirm that all the information provided is accurate and complete to the best of your knowledge.

Signature: _____   Date: _____

Please mail this completed form to:

Returning Citizens Association
490 Lake Park Ave #10552
Oakland, CA 94610
510-872-2832

Email: rca@returningcitizensassoc.org | Website: www.returningcitizensassoc.org

WE APPRECIATE YOUR FEEDBACK

This form is intended for people who are currently incarcerated

Name:

Age:

Ethnicity:

Prison/Jail Number:

Address:

Length of Sentence:

Family Connections (if any):

Mentorship Interest:

Would you like to see more interactive quizzes like this in future issues?
If yes, what types of information or topics would you like included?

Any other feedback or suggestions for Tapped-In Magazine?

Please mail your responses to:
Returning Citizens Association
490 Lake Park Avenue #10552
Oakland, CA 94610

Upcoming Events and Initiatives

Exciting Programs and Milestones for RCA in 2025

Tapped-In Magazine Exhibition and Book Fair (Spring & Summer 2025)

RCA is hitting the road with the Tapped-In Magazine Exhibition and Book Fair, a traveling event celebrating the power of storytelling, education, and resilience. Join us as we travel across major cities to spread awareness and inspire change through stories that matter. This event will bring together system-impacted authors, community organizations, and second-chance advocates to showcase their work and connect with the public. The exhibition will feature:

- Book signings by system-impacted authors.
- Tapped-In Magazine displays and subscriptions.
- Workshops on creative writing and publishing.
- Networking opportunities with reentry advocates and organizations.

RCA's Groundbreaking Life Skills Class Graduation (April 2025)

Graduation is not just an end—it's a new beginning for participants who are reclaiming their lives and shaping their futures. In early April, RCA will celebrate the graduation of participants from our Groundbreaking Life Skills Class. This transformative program equips system-impacted individuals with essential skills for personal and professional growth, including:

- Financial literacy.
- Employment readiness.
- Emotional resilience.
- Communication and conflict resolution.

Youth Mentorship Program Expansion

We're excited to see the next generation thrive with the guidance and support they need to reach their full potential. Our Youth Mentorship Program continues to grow, with RCA facilitators now working in high schools across multiple states. This program focuses on empowering students, particularly those affected by the justice system, by providing:

- One-on-one mentorship with experienced RCA mentors.
- Workshops on resilience, leadership, and goal-setting.
- Tools to align values, attitudes, and behaviors for long-term success.

Tapped-In Magazine: Third Edition (Fall 2025)

The third edition of Tapped-In Magazine is already in production and promises to bring even more impactful stories and resources to our readers. Highlights will include:

- A deep dive into entrepreneurship opportunities for system-impacted individuals.
- Features on second-chance employers making a difference.
- Expanded resources for families and community organizations.
- Success stories from RCA program graduates.

Stay Connected

RCA is committed to driving change, uplifting communities, and amplifying voices. Together, we're building a brighter future—one story, one step, and one initiative at a time. To stay updated on these events and initiatives, visit our website at **www.returningcitizensassociation.org** and follow us on social media.

Acknowledgments

We couldn't have done it without you.

The 2nd Edition of Tapped-In Magazine stands as a testament to the collective effort, passion, and resilience of the incredible individuals who bring the Returning Citizens Association (RCA) to life. This edition was made possible by the dedication of our team, contributors, and supportive community who work tirelessly to empower system-impacted individuals and their families. We extend our deepest gratitude to everyone involved in making this publication a reality.

Our Creative Design Partner
A special thank you to Lacey Kilgrove and her organization, Curated by the Collective, for their exceptional design and creative vision. Lacey's artistry has brought this magazine to life, ensuring it captures the strength, beauty, and resilience of the stories within.

Our Leadership Team
RCA is powered by an extraordinary team of leaders who bring passion, experience, and unwavering commitment to everything they do:

- Richard Gaines, Executive Director, Facilitator, Mentor, and Leader
  Your vision, leadership, and dedication to empowering system-impacted individuals serve as the foundation of RCA's mission.
- Andrea Gaines, Treasurer, Mentor, and Facilitator
  Your steady guidance in managing RCA's resources and your commitment to mentoring others are invaluable to our success.
- Denise Coleman, Project Director
  Your expertise and compassion in addressing mental health challenges continue to create lasting change in our community.
- Marcus Sanders, Project Director and Youth Coordinator
  Your work in mentoring youth and building programs that empower the next generation is inspiring and transformative.
- Anthony Partee, Project Director of the Building Resilience Series
  Your leadership in creating impactful events is vital to spreading RCA's message of resilience and hope.
- Ramon Day, Project Director and Event Coordinator
  Your dedication to planning and executing meaningful events strengthens RCA's community impact.

Our Core Team and Contributors
We are deeply grateful to the amazing individuals who contribute their time, talent, and expertise to RCA and Tapped-In Magazine:

- Robert Montaz, Facilitator and Mentor
  Your guidance and mentorship provide essential support to those navigating reentry. Thank you for your dedication.

- Erica Muniz, Facilitator and Administrative Manager
  Your organizational skills and commitment to creating meaningful change ensure RCA's programs run seamlessly.
- Selma M., Facilitator and Mentor
  Your empathy and mentorship play a critical role in empowering individuals and guiding them toward success.
- Nina Clark, Community Liaison and Secretary
  Your tireless efforts in connecting RCA with the community and ensuring our operations are smooth are invaluable.
- Chop Chop Tan Tan, Project Director of the RCA Zen Garden
  Your vision for creating spaces of peace and healing inspires us all. We love you and appreciate your work.
- Jesse Pitts, Los Angeles Chapter Project Director
  Your leadership in expanding RCA's mission to Los Angeles builds new pathways for impact.
- Wonderful Davidson, Elder Member and Spiritual Leader
  Your wisdom and advocacy for children, especially young girls of color, remind us of the importance of nurturing the next generation.
- Brian Tomasello, Project Director
  Your dedication continues to inspire and we cherish your contributions.
- Jose Ramirez, Mentor and Newest RCA Member
  Your unwavering commitment to resilience, purpose, and faith is a shining example of what RCA stands for.

Our University Interns

A huge thank you to our exceptional RCA interns—university students who bring fresh ideas, energy, and passion to our programs. Your contributions are vital to RCA's success, and we're proud to have you as part of our team.

To Our Community Partners

We deeply appreciate the universities, foundations, and organizations that support RCA through grants, sponsorships, donations, and partnerships. Your belief in our mission confirms the importance of this work and empowers us to continue making a difference in the lives of system-impacted individuals and their families. Your support of RCA and your own efforts to drive real change help us amplify voices that need to be heard.

To Everyone Who Has Supported Us On This Journey

You are part of something bigger. Together, we are reclaiming lives, rewriting narratives, and building a future filled with hope and possibility. Thank you for your dedication, belief in our mission, and the unwavering support you've shown us. Peace and blessings to everyone.

— The Tapped-In Magazine Team

Reader Reflections

The launch of Tapped-In Magazine was a milestone for our team, a platform to amplify the voices of system-impacted individuals and celebrate their resilience. The overwhelming response to our debut issue has been humbling, and we're thrilled to share some of the letters we've received from readers. Your feedback, encouragement, and stories are what drive us to continue this mission. We've edited this issue to include some of the requests from readers and are always looking for ways to better serve our community.

A Resource for Educators

Dear Tapped-In Team,

I'm a high school teacher working with students who face significant challenges, including the impact of incarceration in their families. Your magazine has been an eye-opener for me. It's given me a new perspective on how to support my students and introduce conversations about resilience, education, and second chances. Have you considered creating educational materials based on your content? I believe they could have a tremendous impact in classrooms like mine.

– Ms. Angela P., Fresno, CA

A Voice for the Unheard

Dear Tapped-In Team,

I was deeply moved by the stories shared in your first edition. As someone who has been personally impacted by the justice system, I've often felt invisible to society. Your magazine gave me a sense of pride and hope—knowing that people like me are reclaiming their stories and thriving. I especially appreciated the article on the importance of resilience. It reminded me that no matter how hard life gets, we can rebuild. Thank you for giving us a platform to be seen and heard.

– Maria T., Oakland, CA

Inspiration for a New Path

Dear Editors,

Reading your first edition was a turning point for me. I've been out of the system for a year, and it's been tough finding my way. The article about second-chance employers gave me the courage to apply for jobs I thought were out of reach. I also want to commend the piece on financial literacy—it's a topic we don't talk about enough. I've started budgeting and working on my credit score thanks to your tips. Please keep sharing practical advice like this!

– James W., Dallas, TX

Highlighting Hope

To the Tapped-In Team,

As a family member of someone currently incarcerated, I cannot express how much this magazine means to me. The stories of resilience and success give me hope for my brother's future. It's easy to feel forgotten in this situation, but Tapped-In reminds us that change is possible and that there is a community rooting for us. Do you plan to feature more resources for families like mine? I'd love to see articles about how we can support our loved ones during and after their incarceration.

– Sophia L., San Antonio, TX

Have Something to Share?

We'd love to hear from you! Whether it's feedback on our latest edition, a suggestion for future topics, or a story you'd like to share, your voice matters to us. Send your letters to **rca@returningcitizensassoc.org** or mail them to:

Returning Citizens Association/Tapped-In Magazine
P.O. Box 562
1735 Robinson St.
Oroville , CA 95965-9998

Capital
Gaines LLC

YOUR STORY MATTERS

WE SPECIALIZE IN PUBLISHING NOVELS, POETRY, MEMOIRS, AND MORE, GIVING EVERY AUTHOR THE OPPORTUNITY TO SHARE THEIR VOICE WITH THE WORLD.

OUR MISSION IS TO EMPOWER INDIVIDUALS WITH A UNIQUE CHANCE TO SHOWCASE THEIR TALENTS.

WITH SILVER, BRONZE, AND GOLD PACKAGES, WE TAILOR OUR SERVICES TO MEET YOUR SPECIFIC NEEDS.

LET'S PUBLISH YOUR WORKS TOGETHER. OUR AUTHORS ARE MORE THAN WRITERS; THEY'RE ARTISTS WITH STORIES THAT DESERVE TO BE HEARD.

"Capital Gaines is the truth. I have been trying to get my book published for four years. I am so grateful" - Robert Craig

Visit **www.capgainesllc.com** to begin your publishing journey.

Purchase these works to support the RCA and system-impacted people.

Tapped-In Magazine Summer 2024

Scan the QR code to purchase the first edition of Tapped-In Magazine.

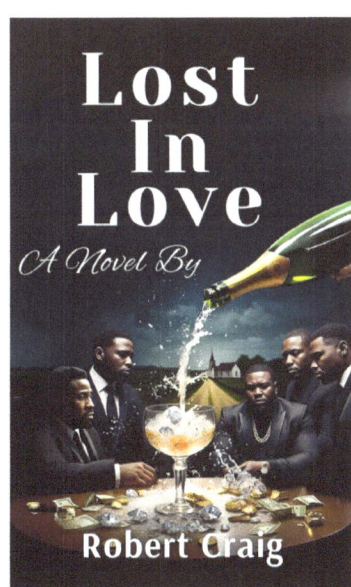

Scan the QR code to purchase *Lost In Love* by Robert Craig

Scan the QR code to purchase *My Advice* by Marcus E. Sanders

We exhibit and sell artworks created within prison walls nationwide. Through art, we work to change the narrative and break the stereotype of what society imagines when thinking about the incarcerated. Visitors to our exhibitions come away with a more nuanced view of the criminal justice system and the need for society to have a vested interest in programs to keep people out of prison and better prepare those who are serving time to successfully reenter society.

 Visit our website to learn more at **escapingtime.org**

justice arts coalition

Justice Arts Coalition (JAC) unites artists impacted by the criminal legal system and creatives everywhere to harness art's transformative power and reimagine justice. Through the sharing of resources, stories, and learning opportunities, JAC is building a nationwide collective of people who are committed to increasing opportunities for creative expression in carceral settings, amplifying the voices of those most impacted by mass incarceration, and shaping public dialogue around the intersection of the arts and justice.

 Visit our website to learn more at **thejusticeartscoalition.org**

IF BLACK WOMEN AREN'T WELL, THE WORLD ISN'T EITHER.

As we look to the future, **empowerHER: Navigating Wellness for Black Women** is poised to grow into an enduring legacy of health and empowerment for Black women—serving as a platform for education, empowerment, and community building, nurturing a legacy that will thrive for generations.

SOAR BLACK GIRL

Empowering **Black Girls and Women** to embrace their full potential, **SousSHE** is a women-led initiative dedicated to fostering creativity, resilience, and leadership. Through culturally-centered programs, we encourage the pursuit of *entrepreneurial, artistic, civic, and holistic dreams*, providing the resources and support needed to thrive.

From cultivating talents in the arts and culinary fields to creating healing spaces for personal growth, **SousSHE** stands at the forefront of advocating for Black girls and women's well-being and success. Join us to share, grow, and be part of a space where every Black woman and girl can see her reflection and thrive.

i.am.sousshe Aspire To Inspire One Girl At A Time

"all she wanted to do was see a reflection of herself."

SousSHE Inc.
248 3rd Street #1250 | Oakland, CA 946057
info@sousshe.org | Tel: (510) 925-5477
soushe.org

California Support Services

Educational Programs

Offering classes in reading and computer literacy, financial literacy, and more to help individuals and families develop essential life skills.

After-School Care

A safe and supportive environment for children to learn, grow, and participate in creative activities outside of school hours.

Mental Health Support

Providing mental health counseling and wellness programs to help individuals manage stress, build resilience, and improve overall well-being.

Parenting Workshops

Guiding parents with resources and strategies to help them create healthy, nurturing homes for their children.

Financial Literacy

Empowering community members with knowledge about budgeting, saving, and planning for a secure financial future.

Reading & Computer Literacy Classes

Offering skill-building classes to improve reading proficiency and computer skills, opening doors to better job opportunities.

Art Classes

Providing creative outlets for expression and personal growth through our art classes.

Housing Assistance for Homelessness

Offering safe, transitional housing to help individuals move towards stability and self-sufficiency.

RETURNING CITIZENS

The Returning Citizens Association (RCA) is an organization dedicated to supporting system-impacted individuals. Our mission is to increase the economic, political, and social capital of returning citizens in the United States. RCA was founded by Richard Gaines, a system impacted individual who understood firsthand the struggles of reentry.

Returning Citizens Association (Established 2022)
EIN 99-4368698
501 (c)(3)
Effective Date 8/2/2024

Visit **www.returningcitizensassoc.org** to learn more.

Creative partnership with Curated By The Collective helped make this magazine possible. Visit **curatedbythecollective.com** to learn more about this community-centered not-for-profit co-op creative agency.